LOFTY AND SKY'S
HAPPY SPACE AND PLACE

STEPH MARQUARDT

ILLUSTRATED BY JESSICA BROPHY

ISBN 979-8-88851-715-4 (Paperback)
ISBN 979-8-88851-716-1 (Digital)

Covenant Books
11661 Hwy 707
Murrells Inlet, SC 29576
www.covenantbooks.com

To all the folks who have endured hardship in becoming parents.
To my miracles, Charlotte and McCoy.
To my unborn children gone too soon.
To Parker, my TLP crews and JC, CT and RS: thank you for believing in me.
To those still longing to be parents, you are not alone.

Romans 15:13

Lofty and Sky live among other giraffes and beautiful creatures in the glorious African savannah.

2

It seems they have everything they need
in their happy space and place,

like tall acacia trees
to crunch and munch.

4

See how their long, dark tongues
nab and grab the twigs and leaves?

5

Sky prefers just the leaves,
if you please.

6

They drink from clean streams and cool pools.

See how Lofty straddles and stoops?

Whoops!

8

They rest and sleep in cozy pockets of shady trees.

See how they sleep and dream?
What do they dream about?

10

Lofty and Sky hope and dream of one lovely thing,

11

to make their space and
place even happier.

12

They long to learn and grow
and have a child of their own.

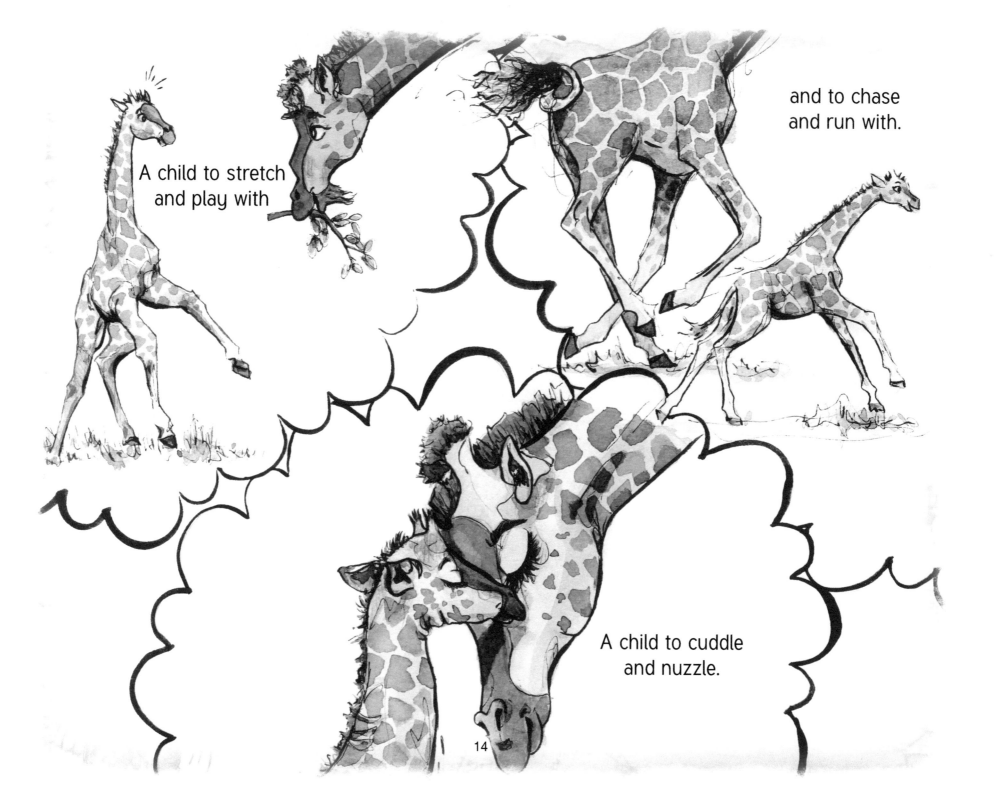

A child to stretch and play with

and to chase and run with.

A child to cuddle and nuzzle.

14

But Lofty and Sky are puzzled and troubled.

15

They dance and sing,

but still no child comes.

They sit and wait quietly,
but still no child comes.

They cry and pray,

19

but still no child comes.

20

And then…

to their joy and delight…

after many seasons of years and tears,

after much help and great hope,

Lofty and Sky welcome home
a child of their own.

Their child to stretch
and play with

and to chase
and run with.

Their child to cuddle and nuzzle.

26

Joy and gratitude came in the shape of a child

27

and filled their happy space and place,

28

AND IT WAS ALL WORTH THE WAIT.

ABOUT THE ILLUSTRATOR

Jessica Brophy was raised on the prairies and mountains of Montana and grew up training horses, raising chickens, and painting. She moved to Los Angeles at the age of eighteen to study interior design for three years. She currently resides in Billings, Montana, with her guinea pig, Coconut, and spends her free time playing music and avoiding cooking.

Jessica owns a business called Free Indeed Art, where she and her assistant artists make custom art. Jessica works one-on-one with each of her clients to create a painting or drawing around their style and what they love. Outside of giraffes, her pet portraits are wildly popular!

Learn more at https://linktr.ee/freeindeedart or follow Jessica on Facebook.

ABOUT THE AUTHOR

Steph Marquardt lives in Montana with Parker and their blended family of four children and two long-haired German shepherds. Steph is a CrossFit coach and part-time Montessori teacher. When she's not writing or at the gym, she enjoys spending time with family, walking the dogs, skiing, hiking, volunteering at church, playing chess, and reading. If she didn't experience motion sickness, Steph would fulfill her Trekkie dreams of becoming an astronaut and go boldly where no one has gone before.

Follow Steph on Instagram @steph.marq.writer